T0044910

Summer Is Here!

Mary Garcia
Illustrated by Shane Nagle

Summer is here!
The sky is so blue.
ST

Summer is here!
There's so much to do.

Summer is here!
We go to the pool.

Pool

Summer is here!
The water is **COOL**!

Lifeguard

Summer is here!
The sun is so **HOT**!

Summer is here!
We find a shady spot.